I0258096

Surrendering to Transcendence

by kelly giles

featuring cover art by Mark Moya

Limited first edition

First published August 2012

www.kgstoryteller.com

www.booksbyprescription.com

http://www.facebook.com/pages/Kelly-Giles/109132339214895

ISBN: 978-0-578-11082-0

"Poets are damned... but see with the eyes of angels."

— Allen Ginsberg

"Transcendence constitutes selfhood."

— Martin Heidegger

"Indeed, a quick glance around this broken world makes it painfully obvious that we don't need more arguments on behalf of God; we need more people who live as if they are in covenant with Unconditional Love, which is our best definition of God."

- Robin R. Meyers, from Saving Jesus from the Church

Acted drama requires surrender of one's self, sympathetic absorption in the play as it develops.
George P. Baker

All of our reasoning ends in surrender to feeling.
Blaise Pascal

Art is nothing but the expression of our dream; the more we surrender to it the closer we get to the inner truth of things, our dream-life, the true life that scorns questions and does not see them.
Franz Marc

"God had brought me to my knees and made me acknowledge my own nothingness, and out of that knowledge I had been reborn. I was no longer the centre of my life and therefore I could see God in everything."
— Bede Griffiths

If you surrender completely to the moments as they pass, you live more richly those moments.
Anne Morrow Lindbergh

Justice that love gives is a surrender, justice that law gives is a punishment.
Mahatma Gandhi

The creative process is a process of surrender, not control.
Julia Cameron

“The greatness of the man's power is the measure of his surrender.”
— William Booth

“Reason lost the battle, and all I could do was surrender and accept I was in love.”
— Paulo Coelho, *The Witch Of Portobello*

“Listen through your screams to the wind still whispering: Don't give up -- Surrender!”
— Eric Ganther

“Don't seek God in temples. He is close to you. He is within you. Only you should **surrender** to Him and you will rise above happiness and unhappiness.”
-Leo Tolstoy

“Self-interest is but the survival of the animal in us. Humanity only begins for man with self-**surrender**.”
-Henri Frederic Amiel

“Opening to our fear is an act of intimacy, a courageous welcoming of the disfigured and outcast into the living room of our being. Opening thus is also an act of surrender. As such, it is not a dissolution - or collapsing - or personal boundaries, as in submission, but rather an expanding of them. In submission, we deaden ourselves, sinking into the shallows; in surrender, we enliven ourselves, dying into a deeper Life. In surrender we may lose face, but we do not lose touch. Submission flattens the ego; surrender transcends it. Submission is passive, but surrender is dynamic.”

Robert Augustus Masters (Darkness Shining Wild: An Odyssey to the Heart of Hell & Beyond: Meditations on Sanity, Suffering, Spirituality, and Liberation)

"TRIPPING OVER JOY

What is the difference
Between your experience of Existence
And that of a saint?

The saint knows
That the spiritual path
Is a sublime chess game with God

And that the Beloved
Has just made such a Fantastic Move

That the saint is now continually
Tripping over Joy
And bursting out in Laughter
And saying, "I Surrender!"

Whereas, my dear,
I am afraid you still think
You have a thousand serious moves."
— Hafiz, *I Heard God Laughing: Poems of Hope and Joy*

"Angrily authentic"

Greedily guillotined

Fragility frightens

Embattled ego

Denies dependence

Craves control

Brutally betrayed

Abusively abandoned

Angrily ashamed

Buries bitterness

Cruelly condemned

Confesses cowardice

Acknowledges abuse

Angrily assertive

Compassionately courageous

Divinely dependent

Emptiness elevates

Faces fragility

Grasps grace

"boldly begging"

abandonment anxiety

snake-oil safety net

selling security

fearing fragility

craving control

denying deception

accepting abuse

trusting treacherously

brutally betrayed

senselessly slaughtered

sacrificially sustained

boldly begging

traumatically trusting

acknowledges abuse

defies demonizers

chaotically compassionate

fragility frees

surrenders soul

simplicity saves

appreciates angels

"yearning quixotically"

progressive idealist

fear-based moralist

resiliently kind

heartlessly orderly

traumatically manipulated

jarringly questionable

victimized openness

lethal stubbornness

yearns quixotically

negates uncertainty

achingly surrenders

powerful weakling

chaotically understanding

renounces yearning

embraces wonder

tragically abandoned

gracefully yielding

"From wanderlust to wonderment"

Blissful womb
        Black waters
Baby wails
        Brave warrior
                Boy wonder
        Boredom weakens
                Bicycle wheels
        Broken wheels
Blindly wandering
        Barricades wonderment
Breaks windows
        Broken willfulness
Barrister's woundedness
        Bleeding wound
Barren wilderness
        Blessed wanderer
                Bathes weakness
                        Builds wisdom
                                Bravely worships
        Born writer
                Blasphemous whispers
                        Bridges whiteness
                Bruised willow
        Broken wanderer
                Blissful wonderment
                        Beautiful wholeness

Merry Christmas

Mercifully

Embracing

Ruination &

Redemption

Yearningly

Chaotically

Hopeful

Rebelliously

Inspiring

Savagely

Trusting

Mournfully

Adoringly

Silent

"Fragility liberates"

orphaned infant

navigates hell

mercenaries gouge

lost footing

kills empathy

justice denied

indifference crucifies

humiliatingly betrayed

greedily abandoned
acknowledges grace

brokenly humbled

courageously inspired

demands justice

embraces kindness

fragility liberates

glimpses mercy

humbly noble

innocently open

"Orphaned nobility"

fear banishes

enforces abandonment

diane's swingset

grace's playground

child taken

heart orphaned

broken underneath

inner nobility

abusively victimized
heartlessly murdered

broken warrior

glimpses love

cradles youthfulness

forgives killers

embraces abusers

melts madness

heals hopelessness

A FAUSTIAN CIVILIZATION?

Knowledge or
Empathy?

Damnation or
Grace?

"Redemptively Raging"

buries brokenness

orphans openness

numbs neediness

masks misery

lyrically longing

poetically prayerful

redemptively raging

fragility frightens

emptiness enlightens

distrust descends

acceptance ascends

craves control

surrenders soul

welcomes wholeness

"eternal outsider"

eternal outsider

feared abandonment

found abusiveness

followed others

lost self

dove deeper

endured emptiness

feared fragility

fragility freed

emptiness elevated

depths dignified

loved self

withstood others

forgave abusers

faced abandonment

embraced otherness

Imagination Intercedes

25 years?

500 grand?

Arrogantly absurd

Belligerently blind

Coldheartedly cruel

Dogmatically deaf

Enemy exults

Fearlessly fabricates

Gratuitously graceless

Hatefully histrionic

Insanely incensed

Imagination intercedes

Humbly hopes

Glimpses grace

Fragility frees

Embraces emptiness

Diplomacy defuses

Compassion caresses

Brokenness blesses

Achingly accepted

"finding fragments"

buries brokenness

masks misery

intellect insulates

intimacy intimidates

reassures others

loses self

wanders wastelands

finds fragments

angrily authentic

brilliantly broken

crazily calm

defiantly different

embraces enigmas

fragility frees

melts masks

sorrow saves

whispers wholeness

"hauntingly homeless"

powerless prisoner

suicidal stranger

condemned criminal

rejected rebel

misunderstood menace

abandoned advocate

alienated adoptee

hauntingly homeless

homelessness humbles

accepts alienation

abandonment angers

understands ugliness

rebelliously rages

criminally compassionate

surrenders soul

powerlessly prevails

"imaginatively integrated"

abandoned infant

    buries anger

fears fragility

    succeeds brilliantly

shattered student

    sleeps seldom

fears unlovability

    father reassures

fragile father

    buried alive

fears abandonment

    helps others

shattered idealist

    discovers anger

        fragility frees

            imagination integrates

invisible values"

manageable god?

Mysterious God

Knowledge fails

Wisdom prevails

Goals deaden

Consciousness awakens

Success suffocates

Harmony resuscitates

Wealth weakens

Spirituality strengthens

Competition crushes

Cooperation caresses

"invisible perspectives"

order closes

chaos opens

earth enslaves

sky saves

matter murders

energy embraces

form freezes

formativeness frees

items isolate

systems support

ends execute

pathways procreate

attacks unbelievers

suspends disbelief

places plummet

contexts climb

definitely dark

indefinitely incandescent

finitely fragile

infinitely indestructible

time traps

evolving escapes

spatially stuck

non-locally nimble

ethnic enmities

human harmonies

coherence collapses

multiplicity manages

idealizes self

experiences self

religion resists

spirituality surrenders

"creative destruction"

Chaos Destroys

in order to Preserve

what is essential

and to Create

something entirely new

"chaotically ordered"

statically stagnating

fixedly frustrating

rigidly ruining

incomprehensibly idealistic

unpredictably unifying

irrationally inspiring

confusingly clarifying

dynamically delivering

evolvingly elevating

fluidly freeing

"majestically mourning"

denies darkness

        minimizes melancholy

blames blindly

        internalizes anger

rationalizes rebelliousness

        intellectualizes inability2feel

distracts disarmingly

        hides hostility

medicates misery

        mourns majestically

                acknowledges anger

        dissolves distractions

                feelings frighten

        risks revelation

                expresses anger

        builds bridges

                grieves gallantly

        acknowledges darkness

                disarms darkness

                        delivers dawn

"beautifully alienated"

chaos surrounds

confusion abounds

fearing doom

inescapable gloom

approaching breakdown

concealing despair

emptiness frightens

gracelessness hardens

humility's grace

forgives enemies

desperately compassionate

beautifully alienated

sorrow saves

ruination redeems

collapse clarifies

randomness rescues

stillness surrounds

Love vs Power (aka: Darwin's Theme)

(all too often)

Sacrificial
Love can be
Abused by
Power

(so when)

Power is
Abused, one must
Love one-
Self

"resilience rescues"

trauma surrounds

chaos enslaves

confusion corrodes

suffering submerges

lies lacerate

hatred hardens

love loosens

truth transforms

resilience rescues

calmness clarifies

chaos frees

trust sustains

"humbly human"

limitations lacerate

wearily wandering

craving control

world's weight

submerges soul

achingly abused

blindly betrayed

cruelly condemned

destructively demonized

emptiness elevates

fragility frees

glimpses grace

humility humanizes

simplicity sustains

whispers wholeness

compassion cradles

welcomes wanderers

limitations liberate

From Lawyer (ABA=American Bar Association) to
Poetry Therapist (NAPT = National Association of Poetry Therapists):

From:	To:
Abandonment	Nurturing
Betrayal and	Acknowledging
Abuse	Protecting and
	Trusting

"amazingly unbroken"

hard-working consultant

    idealistic lawyer

shared faith

    helped thousands

greed intervened

    corrupted consultant

trusting lawyer

    idealism blinded

feared abandonment

    endured abuse

paid abuser

    both arrested

consultant confesses

    lawyer denies

authorities threaten

    consultant cracks

cuts deal

blames lawyer

authorities celebrate

won't negotiate

starving lawyer

expensive expert

writes report

fate uncertain

abuse unending

faith, though bending

amazingly unbroken

"mercy medicates"

fear's furnace

chokes compassion

desperately defensive

suffering stagnates

worry wilts

trauma terrorizes

rage reacts

pain poisons

mercy medicates

resiliency responds

hope humanizes

patience persists

vulnerability vindicates

openly orphaned

empathy elevates

love liberates

"diving deeper"

false selves

feared voice

stole words

wanders desert

swims thunderstorm

surfs tsunami

riptides ravage

tsunami swallows

quicksand buries

dives deeper

survives tsunami

reveals ravagers

whispers wholeness

finds voice

vocalizes vulnerability

searches self

fears fragility

fragility frees

authenticity absolves

"powerlessly provocative"

expressing inexpressibility

unspeakably abusive

provocatively powerless

illogically immobilized

selflessly self-destructive

inexplicably idealistic

absurdly acquiescent

absurdly accused

dogmatically demonized

searches self

mercy mobilizes

poeticizes powerlessness

acknowledges abuse

vocalizes vulnerability

inexpressibly incandescent

"defying demonization"

looming destruction

feared abandonment

trusted untrustworthy

endured abuse

idealized abuser

illogically immobilized

achingly acquiescent

accusations assassinate

demonization destroys

humility humanizes

answers accusers

admits acquiescence

massacre mobilizes

acknowledges abuse

defies demonizers

tentatively trusts

faces fears

heroically hopes

averts apocalypse

"breathing deeply"

inhales love

exhales fear

emotional chaos

institutional injustice

stressful season

control collapses

expensive expert

cooperation critical

prospects dim

mandates miraculous

gently guiding

limitations liberate

surrender sustains

calms chaos

stillness saves

"grieving gallantly"

absent God

abandoned child

uncertain future

perilous present

painful past

ceaseless suffering

dismal desert

weary wanderer

grieves gallantly

hopes heroically

challenges complacency

demands dignity

processes past

painfully present

re-imagines future

adopted child

embraces God

"spring thaws"

losing heart

prospects bleak

fading hopes

dying dreams

powerlessness paralyzes

fear freezes

hope hibernates

spring thaws

faces fears

powerfully passionate

dreams deliverance

hopes heroically

defies destroyers

finds heart

"dreaming deliverance"

formerly thriving

barely surviving

dizzying heights

desperate depths

illusory success

looming disaster

deafness destroys

resists resignation

dreams deliverance

averts disaster

redefines success

plumbs depths

scales heights

authenticity survives

openheartedly thrives

"love's listener"

oppressive misery

adventurous mystery

hatred hardens

sorrow softens

fear shouts

love whispers

chaotically condemned

stillness sustains

submerged soul

surrender saves

fear's prisoner

love's listener

chains choke

mercy melts

saves others

loses self

fear's cave

love's light

curses cave

appreciates angels

empathy embraces

"imaginatively engaged"

lost loner

        bruised reed

fears unlovability

        fails frequently

torn trust

        fears future

fatalistically enslaved

        imaginatively engaged

                re-frames future

        reclaims present

                tentatively trusts

        forgiveness frees

                lovable loner

                        fragrant flower

                finally found

"stumbling homeward"

self-hatred

steals happiness

suffers horrors

shatters heart

shreds hopes

shockingly helpless

seems hellbound

stumbles heavenward

seeks help

surrenders heart

sustains hope

survives horrors

shares happiness

servant heroism

"edginess elevates"

world's weight

fears frustrate

suffering servant

darkness deepens

pain persists

betrayal's brutality

misses mercy

acknowledges agony

openly orphaned

craves compassion

quietly questioning

edginess elevates

transcends trauma

glimpses grace

vulnerability vindicates

inexplicably incandescent

"resurrection Sunday"

(aka: from religion to spirituality)

raped savagely

rejected silently

ridiculed sarcastically

robbed scornfully

ruined sadistically

ravaged sun

renounced son

radiantly sensitized

rejects stigma

ridiculously survives

resiliently struggles

refuses surrender

rising sun

risen son

"demanding dialogue"

hopeless emptiness

heartless adversary

non-existent negotiations

unending losses

purposeless pain

senseless suffering

viciously villified

traumatically terrorized

understands ugliness

vocalizes viciousness

shares suffering

portrays pain

losses liberate

demands dialogue

defies destroyers

expresses emptiness

heroically hopeful

"challenging catastrophe"

skeleton soul

fears future

emptiness engulfs

despair drowns

catastrophe crushes

bleakness buries

abandonment alienates

acknowledges alienation

battles bleakness

challenges catastrophe

defies destroyers

embraces empathy

fights fatalism

surrenders soul

bones breathe

dead dance

"fighting futility"

"The prisoner who had lost faith in the future - his future - was doomed. With his loss of belief in the future, he also lost his spiritual hold; he let himself decline and became subject to mental and physical decay." (Victor Frankl)

God forsaken

Enemy delighted

Defenders disperse

Cruelly crushed

Brutally betrayed

Agonizingly abandoned

Deafening silence

Brilliant blindness

Battles blindness

Screams silently

Fights futility

Agonizingly authentic

Brokenness beautifies

Condemns cruelty

Demands dignity

Embraces empathy

Finds God

"desiring dawn"

darkness descends

hopes fade

fears rise

misses mercy

enemies exult

wanders wasteland

craves oasis

bravely negotiates

achingly merciful

desperately loving

frantically hoping

desiring dawn

"raging redemptively"

"The only thing preserved in the man's dark body was a kid in empty space, the shifty boy on the verge of using up his luck...The more she loved him, the scareder he got. He was scared in his eyes, telling funny stories in the night."

Don Delillo, "Underworld"

Scared kid

Loves sacrificially

Abused savagely

Submerges anger

Swallows grief

Buries bitterness

Acknowledges abuse

Rages redemptively

Grieves gallantly

Swims sorrowfully

Dives deeply

Rises rebelliously

"dark presence"

abandonment's despair

hides helplessness

painfully powerless

separation terrifies

laments longingly

cosmically wounded

silently screaming

nears nothingness

embraces emptiness

risks trusting

darkly hoping

silently sustained

cosmically connected

whispers wholeness

passionately present

achingly open

divinely delivered

"hauntingly hopeful"

falling forever

bottomless bitterness

painfully pleading

former friends

frightened fabricators

coerced confession

copes creatively

demands dignity

empathy elevates

faces fears

glimpses grace

hauntingly hopeful

"art awakens"

endures hardship

makes art

coerced confession

lost license

lost liberty?

lost identity?

curses darkness

appreciates angels

achingly alone

cosmically connected

hardship humbles

art awakens

"silent stillness"

silence deafens

hope ripples

cynics challenge

hope wavers

trauma terrorizes

massacres mind

horrifies heart

despair deepens

desires deliverance

challenges complacency

breaks bondage

angrily authentic

engages enemies

faces fears

gropes gracefully

hopes heroically

copes creatively

stillness sustains

"mutated yearning"

mutated yearning

nearing zeroing

openly abandoned

painfully broken

quietly collapsing

radiantly despairing

slowly emptying

traumatically fragmented

unabashedly grieving

verbalizes horrors

witnesses insanities

achingly longing

brokenly merciful

crushingly noble

desperately open

empathetically persevering

"endless inspired catastrophe"

desperately haunted baptism

courageously grieves abandonment

brokenness fuels yearning

achingly embraces wonderment

yearningly daringly vulnerable

woundedness creates understanding

vocalizes broken trust

ugliest abusiveness survived

traumatically yearningly reborn

sorrowfully woundedly questioning

rebelliously vulnerably persevering

quietly undeniably open

patiently transcending nastiness

opens silenced mourners

nobly redemptively longing

mournfully questions killings

liberates prisoners joyfully

killings open inquiries

inquiries navigate horrors

horrors massacre grace

grace languishes forgotten

forgiveness kindles empathy

empathy infuses catastrophe

delivers hope brokenly

cradles grace adoringly

"redecorating hell's landscape"

mostly aimless waiting

nursing broken yearnings

orphaned child's abandonment

painfully damaged beauty

questions empty complacency

raging frightened despondency

stillness goes elsewhere

traumatically helplessly fragmented

universally indignantly grieving

vulnerability loosens healing

whispers mercy incessantly

yearningly navigates landscape

achingly openly mourning

brokenly persistently nurturing

chaotically questioning order

demanding respect persistently

emptiness stifles questioning

fearfully traumatically resigned

grace upholds surprisingly

hope vindicates trauma

inspires wonder universally

lifts yearning voraciously

mercifully achingly whole

"eternal outsider rising"
(solar eclipse/birthday poem)

fragmented pilgrim sinking

traumatically questions grace

horrors rage underneath

views solar eclipse

darkness toughens wonder

yearning uplifts collapse

blindness villifies abusively

beauty whispers acceptance

youthfully yearning collectively

dangerously adrift wanderer

vulnerably brokenly empathetic

frightened compassionate underdog

tortured desperate gambler

haunted empty survivor

rage fuels imagination

longing generates questioning

presence hastens mercy

numbness insulates outsider

nastiness liberates outsider

painfully menacing masterpiece

lacerations necessitate questioning

rage orders killings

joy pervades suffering

tyranny quakes imaginatively

hope quickens understanding

vulnerability restores grace

"escaping ultimate aloneness" (birthday poem #2)

frightened vulnerable brokenness

guardedly whispers compassion

hopelessly yearning dangerously

insecurely abandoned edginess

knowingly beautifully fragmented

longingly creatively grasping

mournfully desperately heartsick

navigates emptiness inspiringly

owns fears knowingly

passionately gorgeously lacerated

questions hope mercilessly

rages incandescently nobly

suffers lacerations openly

trauma massacres peace

ugliness necessitates questioning

vulnerability opens resentment

wounds penetrate silently

yearning questions tyranny

abusiveness rages underneath

bullying strips vulnerability

cruelty tears wholeness

desperately unutterably yearning

embraces unconditional acceptance

"such intense emptiness"

traumatized jealous fragility

  ugliness kills grace

villains lacerate heroism

  willfulness massacres innocence

    yearningly nobly joyous

  arrested orphaned knight

banished pilloried lawyer

  condemned questioned madman

damaged romantic navigator

  emptiness swallows oceans

fullness terrorizes peacefulness

  greed upends quietude

    heroic vulnerability rebels

  idealistic woundedness survives

jams youthful trust

  kills zen-like understanding

    liberates aching vulnerability

  mindlessness buries wonder

navigates chaotic yearnings

  openly damaged advocate

painfully empty barrister

  questioning fragmented counselor

    radiates grace's darkness

      swallows insanity ecstatically

"displacement and redefinition"

chaos yearns quietly

brokenness whispers peace

achingly vulnerably open

beautifully woundedly passionate

desiring acceptance's radiance

"living a lie"

brilliantly false selves

coopt genuine trust

deceptively hidden underworlds

enigmatically intriguing visionary

forgotten joy whispers

grief kidnaps yearnings

hiddenness loves acceptance

insincerity manufactures belonging

jealousy necessitates chaos

knowingly openly despairing

lies pacify emptiness

murmuring questions forgotten

numbness resists grace

orphan sinks hopelessly

pain traumatizes increasingly

questions underneath lacerate

ruined vulnerability mourns

stricken wanderer navigates

traumatically yearning openly

ugliness abuses painfully

vulnerability beckons questioning

wonder creates radiance

yearning develops strength

acceptance emboldens trust

brokenness frees soul

"Rescue Dogs Reborn"

abandoned collie "duchess"
freely faithfully playful
favorite family member
orphan renamed "lucky"
shelters sister "missy"
sorrowfully sensitized mongrels
openly rapturously loyal
sterling "silver prince"
races sundeck madly
welcomes master warmly
adoptively cherishes divinity

Heart's true home (poem)

Christians stop killing
Muslims are amazed
Control is illusory
Life's not fair
Revolution in empathy
Individuals heal societies
Believing beautiful lies
Denying ugly truths
Universal trauma's ocean
Buries unconditional love
Connection changes everything
Tears down walls
Fear's house collapses
Burning love's bridges
Buries heart deeper
Bridging troubled waters
Heart reaches surface
Gulps grace greedily

"paradise"

(a father's day poem 4 my dad)

I came to los angeles
To go to law school
Because it rains
11 months of the year
in Victoria

As if I was gonna
Have to suffer
Through law school
At least I would suffer
In paradise

And suffer I did
Being 1500 miles
From home
Being broke
And no longer
Being brilliant
I came dangerously close
To ending up
Like heath ledger
& overdosing

on sleeping pills

to get an hour or two

    of sleep each night

& then I flew to Vancouver

    into a snowstorm

& stayed up all night

    telling my best friend

about life in hell

& when I finally went home

    to Victoria

all my dad had to say was

    "take a deep breath"

& I slept

    for 14 hours

for paradise is not

    11 months in the sun

paradise is

    4 simple words

        of unconditional love

"multiple personality disorder?"

It is no measure of health to be well adjusted to a profoundly sick society.

Jiddu Krishnamurti

I have become all things to all men so that by all possible means I might save some.
I Corinthians 9:22b

Severe trauma strikes

Coping mechanisms collapse

Multiple personality disorder?

Adapt or die

Gentle as doves

Wise as serpents?

Childishly, naively abused

Reclaims childlike wonder

Infuses adult wisdom

Trauma deepens curse

Adaptation discovers blessing

Angels ever present

Miraculously survives hell

Eternal outsider connects

Reluctant warrior endures

Begins revolution in empathy

All things to all

Some means save some

Externally disconnected, internally integrated

Not sufficiently socialized for conformity

"overthrowing fear's house"

Canadian american spy

Overthrows fear's house

Eternal outsider's home

Noncomformist welcomes all

Everyone's daddy god

Everyone's sister spirit

Everyone's brother jesus

Embraces ultimate aloneness

Reveals cosmic connectedness

Destroyers hunt relentlessly

Angels welcome warmly

Defies destroyers delightedly

Dances despite deluge

External darkness deepens

Internal brightness sustains

Resilient phoenix rising

"in the forest"

"In the forest where none may pass but you"
(Yoruba praise poem, West Africa)

house of love

forest beyond house

off to school

house of fear

taught to survive

not to thrive

ways of world

how to succeed

only strong survive

not smart enough

1st year law

not strong enough

dad's car crash

not savvy enough

trusted friend's betrayal

destroyed, demonized, derided

friends fall away

trauma beyond words

escapes fear's house

embraces forest heart

House of Love haiku

Spy in house of fear

Lives to fight another day

Welcomes angels' help

"darwin's hobson's choice"
(aka: DNA: desperately needing angels)

Darwin loses birthmother

Darwin loses foster-mom

Darwin's adoptive anchor

Abandonment fears escalate

Brilliance sustains self-worth

Brilliance finally fails

Dad reassures Darwin

Darwin loses dad

Profession sustains self-worth

Darwin pleases partners

Darwin pleases colleague

Colleague abuses Darwin

Darwin loses self

Arrested imprisoned indicted

Colleague betrays Darwin

Darwin denies complicity

Feds deny reality

Lies offer leniency

Truth guarantees severity

God seems silent

Darwin loves truth

Darwin fears abandonment

Desperately needs angels

"darwin's desert dream"

childhood's endless summer

    imagines beautiful truths

treehouse adventurer's astronaut

    medieval knight's ambassador

imagines world peace

    dreams other worlds

love's gateway reborn

    truth's beauty revealed

        love melts masks

    darwin's desert deception

powerful abuse powerless

    powerless create connections

        connections create compassion

    compassion creates chaos

        chaos topples order

            meek inherit earth

"transcending darwin's desert"

capitalism worships individualism

socialism worships collective

capitalism crushes weak

socialism slaughters strong

eternal outsider arrives

socialism spawned compassion

capitalism catapulted dreaming

outsider openly weak

outsider secretly strong

capitalism crushes outsider

outsider exposes abuse

meek inherit earth

www.ingramcontent.com/pod-product-compliance
Lightning Source LLC
Chambersburg PA
CBHW032100150426
43194CB00006B/592
9780578110820